Exploring Old Montreal

360
Celebrating Montreal's
Anniversary
1642-2002

Bonsecours Market (330 St. Paul E.) opened in 1846.
The dome has been destroyed by fire three times.

WALKING TOURS OF MONTREAL

Exploring Old Montreal

An Opinionated Guide to the Streets, Churches, and Historic Landmarks of the Old City

Alan Hustak

Véhicule Press

Cover design: David Drummond
Maps: David Widgington
Cover photograph: Alan Hustak
Typeset in Minion by Simon Garamond
Printing: AGMV-Marquis Inc.

Published with the assistance of the Book Publishing Industry Development Program of the Department of Canadian Heritage.

CANADIAN CATALOGUING IN PUBLICATION DATA

Hustak, Alan, 1944-

Exploring Old Montreal

(The walking tours of Montreal)

ISBN: 1-55065-135-8

1. Vieux-Montréal (Montréal, Quebec)–Tours.
2. Montréal (Quebec)–Tours.
3. Walking–Quebec (Province)–Montréal–Guidebooks. I. Title.
II. Series: Hustak, Alan, 1944- . Walking tours of Montréal)

FC2947.52.H88 2000 917.14'28044 C00-900311-8
F1054.5.M86053 2000

Véhicule Press
P.O.B. 125, Place du Parc Station
Montreal, Quebec H2W 2M9

www.vehiculepress.com

Distribution in U.S. by
Independent Publishers Group, Chicago

Printed in Canada.

Contents

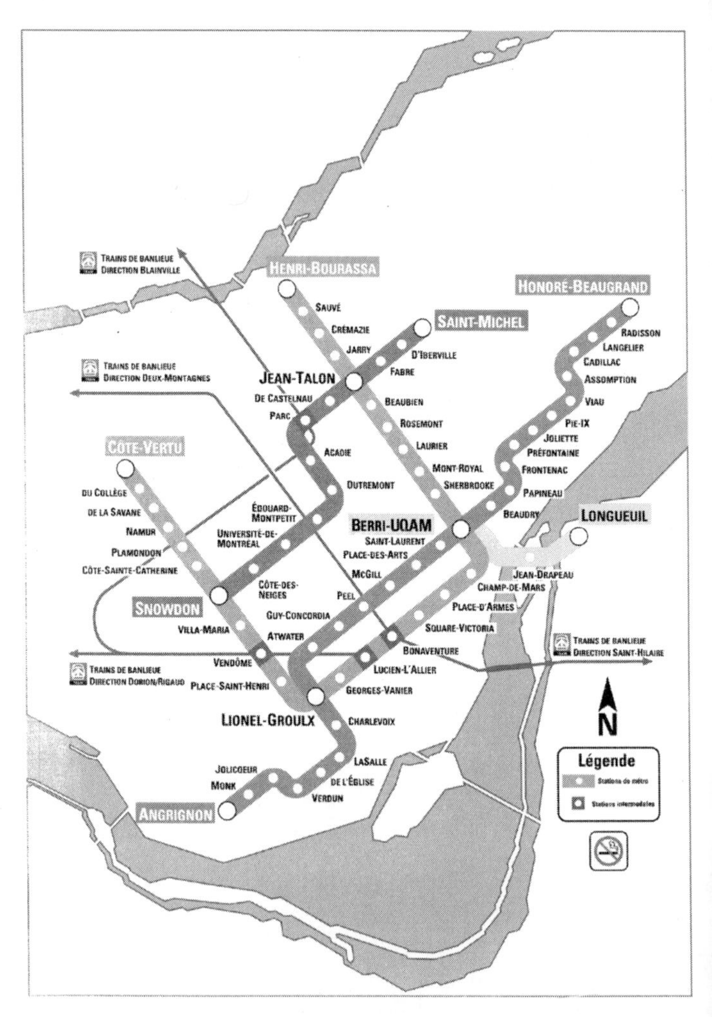

Métro map.
It costs $2.25 cash fare to ride the Métro and buses;
six tickets are $9

Useful Information

TOURIST INFORMATION

Tourist Information Centre of Old Montreal
174 Notre-Dame Street East
(Champ-de-Mars métro)
Maps and brochures, telephone cards, the Museums Pass.
Web site: www.tourism-montreal.org

Infotouriste Centre
1001 du Square-Dorchester Street
(cor.Peel and Ste-Catherine streets / Peel métro)
(514) 873-2015 / 1-800-363-7777
Offers maps and pamphlets on Montreal and Quebec, information on what's on and where to buy tickets, plus bus tours and hotels.
Web site: www.bonjourquebec.com

Post Office
435 St-Antoine W. & 11 Notre-Dame W., (8:00 am-5:45 pm)

ENTERTAINMENT LISTINGS

Montreal is a newspaper town with three French-language dailies—**La Presse, Le Devoir, Journal de Montréal**—and the English-language **Gazette** (particularly the Friday and Saturday editions). Four free entertainment weeklies are published every Thursday—two in French (**Voir** and **Ici**), and two in English (**Hour** and **The Mirror**)—and they all have extensive listings.

Web sites:
Hour – www.hour.qc.ca
Gazette – www.montrealgazette.com
The Mirror – www.montrealmirror.com
Voir – www.voir.ca/mtl.asp
Ici – www.icimontreal.com

RESTAURANTS

Montreal's many restaurants are proof that its citizens love to eat out. Two guides to the culinary diversity of the city are **Cheap Thrills: Great Montreal Meals for Under $15** ($9.95), and **Montreal's Best Restaurants** by Byron Ayanoglu ($14.95).

MONTREAL TRANSIT SYSTEM (STM)

The STM's Web site provides maps and schedules, in English and French, for the Métro and bus, plus a complete map of the Underground CIty.
Web site: www.stcum.qc.ca

AIRPORTS AND AIRLINES

Aéroport de Montréal – Dorval & Mirabel
(514) 394-7377
1-800-465-1213 (Toll free Canada, Vermont and Albany)
Web site: www.admtl.com
Complete information on both airports including departures and arrivals for all airlines.

AIRPORT BUS SHUTTLE

(514) 931-9002

TRAINS AND INTER-CITY BUSES

Montreal Bus Central Station
505 de Maisonneuve Blvd. East
(514) 843-8495
Berri-UQAM métro

Via Rail Canada - Central Station
895 de la Gauchetière Street West
(514) 989-2626
Bonaventure métro
Web site: www.viarail.ca

Introduction

Montreal is a lot like a multi-layered *pousse café*, you have to take each of its flavours as it comes. You can't really appreciate one layer without sampling the other. That's one of the secrets of its charm.

Montreal is really a number of little villages and Old Montreal is its oldest. Here you will find the spirit of its *ancien regime* survives just below the surface of the modern city that has grown up all around it. There's a nervous edge here, an intellectual sharpness, and an ebullience that few cities on the continent can match, the most obvious exception being New York.

Old Montreal is the classic city, defined by the silver dome of the Bonsecours Market to the west, the spires of Notre Dame Basilica in the centre and the historic Place Royale and Pointe-à-Callières to the west. The area is a compact 90 acres, and as you explore its skinny streets you will find yourself meandering through a cradle of history.

Many of the continents' great explorers who molded a continent have walked these streets: René-Robert Cavelier de LaSalle, who discovered the Mississippi; Sieur de la Vérendrye, the first European to see the Rockies; Antoine de la Mothe Cadillac who founded Detroit in 1701; and Jacques Marquette who opened what is today Illinois, all made Montreal home at one time or another.

Old Montreal packs a great deal into a small area and has been a magnet for pedestrians ever since. You don't want to drive here. Its narrow, twisted streets were designed for horses, not automobiles. If you insist on bringing a vehicle into the old city the most sensible thing to do is park it indoors at Complexe Chaussegros-de-Léry (330 Champ de Mars, 514-878-0750), otherwise you are almost certain to get a parking ticket or your car will be towed away. Most of the parking spots are reserved for residents with permits.

Old Montreal has surprises at every turn. You can touch the foundations of the original mission built in 1642, stroll along rue Chagouamigon, the continent's shortest street with the longest name (Shah-goo-ahm-ee-gone), see where Canada's first Parliament once stood, take a peek at hundreds of antique dolls, or kneel before a saint in a crystal coffin.

History was made here but Old Montreal is no longer the rowdy waterfront marketplace or the Bohemian village that it once was. Since 1995 it has become a smart address. Rents have climbed and lofts, especially one with a river view, have become both desirable and expensive. New apartments and condo conversions have doubled the residential population. In 1976 fewer than 500 people lived in Old Montreal; today, the population is more than 3,000, and most are newcomers.

Parts of Old Montreal aren't all that old either. They just pretend to be. The cobblestone streets that remain go back to 1964 when Old Montreal was made new all over again for Expo 67, the International World's Fair that celebrated Canada's centenary. The first out-door cafes were licensed then and the area was designated the city's Latin quarter. During the summer Olympic Games in 1976, international television camera crews discovered Place Jacques-Cartier and made it instantly recognizable around the world.

The Walking Tours

Montreal's Beaux-Arts-style City Hall viewed from Place Jacques-Cartier. Admiral Horatio Nelson's statue can be seen on the left.

City Hall Area and Points East

To fully appreciate Old Montreal begin your tour of the area in **Place de la Dauversiére**, the small park in front of City Hall (275 rue Notre-Dame E.), which recalls the city's mystical beginnings. The park is named for **Jerome Le Royer de la Dauversière** (1597-1659) a devout, Roman Catholic tax collector from La Flèche, France who, in 1632, had a vision of Montreal. Convinced in a dream that God wanted him to work for the salvation of the Indians of New France, la Dauversière started a secular society to colonize the island. It recruited a career soldier, **Paul de Chomedey de Maisonneuve** who establish the first permanent mission on the island in 1642.

The small, rusty **Dauversière memorial** is well intentioned, but not very practical. It is most effective at night if the reflecting glass panel flush against the ground is working. The monument is meant to be illuminated from below so you can trace the ghostly image of the city as it was laid out in 1650, except, the lights are rarely on.

The statue a few steps below is of **Jean Drapeau**, (1916-1999) another visionary who put the city on the map in the 1960s and 1970s. Drapeau was one of the most popular mayors of any city, anywhere, and he gave Montreal some of its happiest moments—the Expo 67 World's Fair and the 1976 Summer Olympic Games. Appropriately Annick Bourgeau's statue of Drapeau is beside City Hall beneath the office he occupied for 29 years.

Montreal's City Hall (Hôtel-de-Ville) is a reconstruction

The Château Ramezay, across from City Hall, was built in 1705 as a mansion for Montreal's 11th governor.

of another city hall that opened in 1878 on the same spot and was inspired by the Hôtel-de-Ville in Paris. Designed by **Henri-Maurice Perrault** and **Alexander Cooper Hutchison** in the Second Empire Beaux-Arts style, the original building was gutted by fire in 1922, but its exterior walls were saved. When city hall was rebuilt an additional storey and the tower were added.

The balcony over the main entrance is a historic spot. French **President Charles de Gaulle** gave credence to the Quebec separatist movement when, in 1967 he delivered his provocative declaration, "Vive le Québec libre."

Go up the steps, past two sculptures and into the **Great Hall of Honour.** The big statues in the vestibule are by renowned Quebec sculptor **Alfred Laliberté**; the figure on the right is called "The Seeder," the one on the left is "Woman Carrying a Bucket." Both are rural images of a Quebec long since past. Beyond the vestibule is the ceremonial hall of honour, a vast room of gilded bronze fixtures and Corinthian columns. The floor is laid out in a symmetric design in marble imported from the French Pyrenees. On the south wall are bronze busts of two of the city's mayors, **Jacques Viger** the first French- speaking mayor (1833-36), and **Peter McGill**, the city's first English-speaking mayor (1840-1842).

During the 19th century and up until 1914, the mayor's office alternated between French and English. In the 20th century, the city has was ruled by three so called "boss" mayors, who dominated municipal politics for more than two thirds of the century: Médéric Martin (1914-1928), Camillien Houde (1928-1954), and Jean Drapeau, (1954-1986). Portraits of 39 of the city's 40 mayors are in the corridors surrounding the great hall of honour.

In January 2002 all of the municipalities on the island of Montreal were merged into one city and the first mayor of the newly created megacity is **Gérald Tremblay**, a Harvard-educated corporate lawyer and former Quebec cabinet minister. Tremblay presides over a 73-seat council, whose chambers are just off the Hall of Honour. Forty of those councillors represent districts in what used to be Montreal, the other 33 represent the surrounding suburban city boroughs.

Originally the stained glass windows in the chamber were to have featured portraits of the island's founders, but the windows installed in 1928 instead commemorate, from left to right, the city's religions, agriculture, commerce, industry, and transportation.

Almost directly in front of city hall is the **Château Ramezay** (280 Notre-Dame East, 514-861-8317). It was built in 1705 as a mansion for Montreal's 11th governor, **Claude de Ramezay** (1659-1724) and is the finest public building in Old Montreal that survives intact from the *ancien* or French regime. Designed in the French château style by **Pierre Courturier**, the building has 15 interconnecting rooms. The ballroom, today known as the **Salles des Nantes**, was added around 1830. The mirrored and mahogany-paneled room is so named because the carved wall panels come from a building once owned by the Companie des Indes in the seaport of Nantes, France. To commemorate the ties, the rare wood was given to Canada as a centennial gift by France in 1967 and installed in the château. Ramezay went broke trying to maintain the residence. The French colonial trading company bought the property from the Ramezay family in 1742, moved its corporate headquarters to Montreal and enlarged the building. After the British arrived in Montreal in 1760 the Château became the residence of the Governors-General of British North America. During the American Revolution the U.S. Continental Army seized the building and both American Generals **Richard Montgomery** and **Benedict Arnold** used it as American headquarters in Canada.

It remained a governor's residence until 1844, then was used variously as a courthouse, a college of medicine, and as a normal school. Both French-language newspapers, *La Presse* and *La Minervre* had their offices in the building. In 1895 it was sold to the Antiquarian and Numismatic Society of Montreal who have run it as a museum ever since. The turrets that gives it the idealized appearance of a French Château weren't added until 1903.

In 1929 Château Ramezay was the first building in Quebec to be declared a national historic monument. The museum has one of the largest collections of early

The small formal garden behind the Château Ramezay.

Canadian art and furniture. Among the 20,000 pieces in its collection are the Louisbourg bell, installed in the chapel at Fortress Louisbourg in 1724; James Morgan's portrait of **Benjamin Franklin** (who was once a guest at the Château); and the **first automobile** ever driven in the city, an 1898 Dion-Bouton owned by the Dandurand family.

The Château Ramezay museum just re-opened following a period of renovation and restoration. The small formal garden behind the museum recreates, on a small scale, three gardens that existed on the grounds in the 18th century—a formal pleasure garden and fountain, a vegetable garden, and an orchard.

Two blocks east of the château is the **Sir George-Etienne Cartier National Historic Site** (458 Notre-Dame E.,514-283-2282). Cartier (1814-73) was one of the Fathers of Canadian Confederation and twice in his distinguished career made the greystone house his residence. The museum offers excellent insight into the life of a wealthy Victorian politician as costumed guides bring the 19th century to life.

Along the way to Cartier House you will cross Bonsecours Street. On your right is the Sailor's **Chapelle Notre-Dame-de-Bonsecours** (Our Lady of Perpetual Help). The 400-seat chapel is not, as many guide books tell you the oldest church in Montreal, but it stands on the foundations of a church built on the site in 1657 by **Marguerite Bourgeoys,** (1620-1700) who was made a saint in 1982. A small stone chapel replaced the original she had built in 1675, but it burned in 1754. The cornerstone for the existing building was laid in 1771.

The facade of the church was rebuilt in 1886 to include the double-bell tower, flanked by two smaller spires. A few years later, the elaborate rear extension was added.

As you head down the block towards the church you will pass two historic buildings. The first, halfway down the street on your right, with a double row of 11 dormer windows, is the **Papineau Residence** (440 Bonsecours). It was built in 1785 by John Campbell, then sold to prominent lawyer **Joseph Papineau** (1752-1841). His more famous son, **Louis-Joseph,** (1786-1871) who led the1837 rebellion against the British in Lower Canada, was born there. Architecturally, the house is noteworthy because its exterior walls are wood painted to look like stone. During most of the 20th century it was a flop house and for awhile used as a fish market until it was bought in 1961 by Montreal journalist **Eric McLean** who restored it. McLean was almost single-handedly responsible for stimulating redevelopment and breathing new life into the neighbourhood. He sold the house to the federal government in 1982 but lived in it until his death in 2002. It is expected the house will be converted into a museum.

At the bottom of the street on your left is the **Auberge Pierre du Calvet** (514-282-1725) and the **Maison Calvert**

The landmark statue of Mary on the roof of
Chapelle Notre-Dame-de-Bonsecours, c. 1963

(405 Bonsecours) built in 1770 for **Pierre de Calvet** (1735-1786) a notary who was jailed for treason in 1780 and later banished for life from Montreal for collaborating with the Continental Army during the **American Revolution.** The house was restored in 1966 to mark the centennial of the tony Ogilvy Department store, and acquired by its present owner, Gaëten Trottier, in 1984, who converted the buildings around it into a rustic hotel. The guest rooms and suites are decorated with antiques, family souvenirs and gold framed portraits. The dining room is one of the most elegant rooms in Old Montreal, but the food doesn't always match the magnificent decor. Rooms in the auberge cost around $200 a night.

The Sailor's Chapel, **Chapelle Notre-Dame-de-Bonsecours** directly in front of the Calvet House has been remodeled so many times since it was built between 1771 and 1773 that it's hard to find anything of the exterior that's original. In 1953, the main steeple, which was about 40 metres high, was discovered to be structurally unsound, so some 10 metres of it was indiscriminately lopped off. The inscription in French above the door reads, "If the love of Mary is engraved in your heart, as you pass by don't forget to say a Hail Mary." The chapel inside, with its delicate shades of cream and blue, crystal chandeliers, and coloured glass windows depicting eight scenes in the life of Mary was refurbished in 1998. The ships that hang from the ceiling are votive lamps left behind by sailors in thanksgiving. Mass in the chapel is celebrated in English every Saturday at 4 p.m. between March and December.

An adjoining **museum** (514-282-8670) tells the life story of Bourgeoys, the chapel's founding saint, in 52 minatures featuring dolls and holograms. You can also get into the **crypt** and see the foundations of the original chapel.

The 92 steps to the ariel chapel and observation tower are popular with children. From the top there is a panoramic view of Old Montreal and the harbour and Ile Ste. Hélène.

The huge statue of Mary on the roof with the aureole of stars around her head is believed to be the only work of craftsman **Philipe Laperle.** It is about 10 metres high, weighs six tonnes and was installed in 1894. The landmark statue has been venerated by pilgrims, admired by tourists, and even celebrated in the song "Suzanne" by Montreal poet **Leonard Cohen:** "and the sun pours down like honey on our lady of the harbour." As Cohen once explained: "Our lady of the harbour is the church and she is Suzanne, and she is the Virgin, and she is the mistress of rescue and protection. You can see her two gold angels overlooking the river."

The colossal greystone building with the silver dome in the block immediately west of the church is **Bonsecours Market** (330 St-Paul E.), the commercial heart of Old Montreal. When it opened in 1846 the market was considered one of the country's most impressive buildings. It is 535 feet long and the dome 100 feet high and 45 feet in diameter. When Bonsecours Market opened, only Boston's Faneuil Hall Marketplace could match its scale and grandeur. With its impressive white Doric columns, Bonsecour Market owes its Classic Grecian Victorian style to British architect **William Footner**. The building sprawls across a city block and covers 100,000 square feet on three floors—about the size of two football fields. It is patterned after the Customs House in Dublin. Even before construction was completed, the Canadian Parliament used the building for its session in 1849 when Montreal was the capital of Canada. Between 1852 and 1878 the market also housed Montreal's city hall, and was used as a police station, a library, an armoury,and ball-room. The building was made a civic monument in 1937. The dome has burned three times—in 1942, 1948, and again in 1976. It closed as a market in 1964, and housed municipal offices until it was renovated and revitalized as a commercial shopping mall in 1993.

Today, the market houses 15 upscale **handicraft shops and boutiques** including the Montreal Design Institute and Quebec Craft Gallery (514-397-0666) the Worn Doorstep Boutique (514-397-0666), and Serge Ricchi (514-393-1532).

Across the street from Bonsecours Market, tucked into a courtyard behind the gates you will find the **Auberge Bonsecours** (353 St-Paul E., 514-396-2662), a tiny seven-room inn. The rooms rent for $125 a night (single) to $175 (double).

Kitty-corner to the market is **Rasco's Hotel** (295 St-Paul E.) which opened in 1836. While it was still under construction, the St. Andrew's Society held its founding meeting in the hotel's ballroom "to give aid to fellow Scots in distress." Built by an Italian immigrant, Francisco Rasco, the 80-room hotel was considered the city's finest until Rasco went back to Italy in 1844. The officers of the British Garrison in Montreal made it their club and Charles Dickens was a guest in 1842. After Rasco left, the hotel was run into the ground by a succession of owners until 1960 when it was abandoned. It burned in 1977. The hotel was renovated and now houses government offices. A street named for Dickens disappeared in 1999 when the condo beside the hotel was built. **Bleu**, the restaurant in the hotel (514-861-5337), is worth a visit even if nothing on its eclectic menu appeals to you. You can enjoy a drink on the quiet outdoor terrace in the back.

For more Quebec handicrafts you might want to drop into the boutique **Galerie métiers d'art** (272 St. Paul E.) across the street, which represents more than 70 of the province's leading artisans.

Continue one block west and you will arrive at Place Jacques-Cartier with its outdoor terraces and cafés.

Place Jacques-Cartier

Place Jacques-Cartier has always been visual chaos. A century ago one Montreal newspaper described it as "a pest hole, a place to be shunned" and for many, it seems not much has changed. It is still a carnival of sights and sounds. During most summer evenings street vendors, clowns, musicians, mariachi bands, organ grinders, fiddlers, jugglers, and panhandlers buzz around shoulder to shoulder. Tour buses disgorge hordes of tourists who swarm through like locusts with cameras.

Since the 18th century Place Jacques-Cartier has been the heart of the old town's commercial, social, and administrative activities. The square was named in 1847 to honour the French explorer (1491-1557) who claimed Canada for France in 1535. Originally the square was the formal garden for the **Château Vaudreuil** built in 1723 by the governor of New France, the first **Marquis de Vaudreuil, Philippe de Rigaud**. The château, which stood at the bottom of the square facing the river, burned in 1803. The gardens were bought by two civic-minded members of Quebec's House of Assembly, Jean-Baptiste Amable Durocher and Joseph Perinault. They gave the property to the city for use in perpetutity as a public market which flourished there until the mid 1950s.

The column at the top of Place Jacques-Cartier is the **Nelson Column**. The 10-metre monument is the oldest in the city. It went up in 1809, four years after **Horatio Nelson** routed Napoleon's navy at Trafalgar and 30 years before the famous monument in London's Trafalgar Square. The column itself was completely restored and rededicated by Lord Strathcona on October 20, 1900. Nelson's

Market Day, Place Jacques-Cartier, c.1890 looking toward the Nelson statue and City Hall.

perch in Montreal has always been precarious. Quebec nationalists keep wanting it torn down or moved. A plot to blow it up involving the son of Montreal's police chief was foiled in the 1890s. The most recent flap erupted in 1996 when former Mayor Pierre Bourque wanted to banish the statue from the square altogether. It was, however, refurbished in 1998.

As you start up the square and head towards the monument, you will be walking along what was once Rue St-Charles, one of the oldest streets in the city. It was laid out in 1672 and borders the east side of the square.

Heading north the first two buildings you will pass are the **Maison Parthenay** (401 Place Jacques-Cartier) and **La Maison Cartier** (407 Place Jacques-Cartier), built by two local entrepreneurs who made fortunes during the

War of 1812.

Old Montreal does not just live, it lives outdoors, and tucked in between the Maison Cartier and the Nelson Hotel you will find **Le Jardin Nelson** (514-861-5731), a pleasant, if often overcrowded, outdoor courtyard café. The courtyard is weatherproof; there are huge umbrellas and heating elements to keep it comfortable through rain and chilly evenings. Usually a jazz or classical trio performs as you sip and eat under the shade of a crabapple tree.

The **Nelson Hotel** next door dominates the east side of the square. It was built in 1866 as the Traveller's House. From 1875 to 1880 the Grand Trunk Railway had its head office here. It's been the Nelson since 1941. During the 1960s and 1970s its blue-collar tavern on the ground floor was a popular watering hole for separatists and FLQ terrorists. No longer a hotel, it houses the absolutely non-threatening **Merville Café.** (514-397-0207).

The last building on your right, the Ben & Jerry's ice cream stand is the **Maison Vandelac** and its origins go back to the French regime. The foundations of the stone house were laid in 1654, 12 years after Montreal was founded.

Walk to the middle of the square to get a good look at the **Nelson monument.** The four ornamental panels include a **memorial inscription**, (N) and scenes from Nelson's great naval victories; the Battle of the Nile (W); the Battle of Copenhagen (E); and his death at Trafalgar (S).

The memorial inscription has faded, but it reads in full, "In memory of the right honourable **Vice-Admiral Lord Viscount Nelson**, Duke of Bronté, who terminated his career of Naval glory in the memorable battle of Trafalgar on the 21st of October, 1805, after inculcating by signal this sentiment: England Expects Every Man Will Do His Duty. This monument column was erected by the inhabitants of Montreal in the year 1808."

The inscription below the panel representing the Battle of the Nile reads: "On the First and Second Days of August, 1798, Rear Admiral Sir Horatio Nelson with a British Fleet of 12 sail of the line and a ship of 50 guns defeated in Aboukir Bay a French fleet of 13 sail of the line and 4 frigates without the loss of a British ship."

Reading the next panel you will discover "The Right Honorable Vice-Admiral, Lord Viscount Nelson, Duke of Bronté, after having on the 2nd of April, 1801, with 10 sail of the line and 2 ships of 50 guns, sunk, taken and destroyed the Danish line, moored for the defence of Copenhagen, consisting of 6 sail of the line, 11 ship batteries & supported by the Crown and other batteries, displayed equal precision and fortitude in the subsequent arrangements and negotiations with the government; whereby the effusion of human blood was spared and the claims of his country established."

Nelson's victory and death at Trafalgar are commemorated with the lines: "On the 21st of October, 1805, the British fleet of 27 sail of the line, commanded by the Right Honourable Lord Viscount Nelson, Duke of Bronté, attacked, off Trafalgar, the combined fleets of France and Spain, all 33 sail of the line, commanded by Admirals Villeneuve and Gravina, when the latter were defeated with the loss of 19 sail of the line captured or destroyed. In this memorable action, his country has to lament the loss of her greatest naval hero, but not a single ship."

Overlooked these days is just how much of a hero Nelson was two hundred years ago. Both French and English Montrealers eagerly subscribed to the monument's fundraising campaign. French-speaking Montrealers at the time were, for the most part royalist. The had opposed the revolution in France and chipped in to build Nelson's column because they welcomed the defeat of Napoleon's navy.

A few steps west at the corner of Place Jacques-Cartier and Notre-Dame street is the **Infotouriste Centre** (174 Notre-Dame E.) housed in a building that went up in 1812. For more than a century it was the **Silver Dollar Saloon**, so called because 350 silver dollars were embedded in its floorboards.

As you start to walk along the west side of Place Jacques-Cartier note the building next door at 446 which went up as the **Hotel Riendeau**. When it opened in 1832 it boasted a rooftop pavilion "from which guests can obtain the finest view of the River St. Lawrence." It is also noteworthy because the **Montreal German Society** was founded there in 1835. As the Riendeau it was the mess hall for the British garrison in the 1860s and for most of this century was known as either the Taft or the Iroquois. Many baby boomers remember it as the site of Plexi, one of the first and most popular discothèques in the city. The building was converted into government office buildings in 1980 and **Galerie Le Chariot** (446 Place Jacques-Cartier, 514-875-4994) which specializes in Inuit art moved into its ground floor in 1985.

Continuing south, you will pass **L'Aventure** (514-935-7841)in the old St. Nicholas Hotel, which was constructed in the 1850s, and **Le Fripon** (514-861-1386), in the former Platt building, which went up in 1828.

The narrow alley to your right is **St. Amable Lane**, which is filled with street artists. Much of what is on display is tacky, overpriced, and kitsch reproductions of Montreal streetscapes, but occasionally you might find a bargain.

The stone house at 410 was built in 1815 by Louis Foretier for his daughter, **Marie-Amable**, a shrewd businesswoman who later married **Denis-Benjamin Viger**, a prominent journalist, lawyer and politician. The property was declared a historic site in 1966.

Inside, you'll find the famed **St. Amable** restaurant (410 Place Jacques-Cartier, 514-866-3471) which offers good classic dishes, although the restaurant isn't what it once was and is quite expensive. Attached to the St. Amable is the **Maison del Vecchio**, which opened in 1897 as an inn by one of the first Italian immigrants to Montreal, **Pierre del Vecchio.** It remained in the del Vecchio family until 1946. Canadian Industries Ltd. restored it in 1966 and had a had a short life as a museum before it became **La Marée** seafood restaurant (514-861-8126).

Cross St. Paul Street and you will come to the **Chez Queux** restaurant (158 St. Paul E., 514-866-5194) which is housed in the Wilson Building erected in 1862. The award-winning restaurant is a shrine to classic French gastronomy with a retro-luxe menu and extravagant decor with red velour, heavy chandeliers, and fireplaces. Directly opposite, on the other side of the square is the **Tiffin Building**, designed by William Footner in 1855. He's the same architect who designed the Bonsecours Market. (*See page* 21).

The Courthouse District

You might say that Montrealers are men and women of conviction. There are no less than five court house buildings in the same block as City Hall. The oldest judicial building in the city, the one with the dome immediately to the left of city hall (155 Notre-Dame E.), was designed by **John Ostell** (1813-1892) a prolific architect responsible for many of Montreal's public buildings in the 1840s and 1850s. The courthouse took six years to build and opened in 1856. It is patterned after the main post office in London. The building was enlarged and the cupola added in 1894 was used as a law courts library. The annex on the west side was completed in 1905. The building was used as general headquarters of the organizing committee for the 1976 Summer Olympic Games, and after the games was named the Lucien Saulnier Building to honour a respected civic bureaucrat. It today houses the city's financial planning department.

The imposing building with the fourteen Doric columns immediately across the street at 100 Notre-Dame St. E. is the **Quebec Appeal Court.** It is the city's second courthouse. Designed in the art deco style by **Ernest Cormier** (1885-1980) it opened in 1926. The monumental bronze doors are 25 feet high and 12 feet wide, and weight ten tonnes. The bronze panels elebrate justice and the law. The meaning of the latin inscription across the top of the colonnade, *Frustra legis auxilium quaerit qui in legem committ,* suggests that if you break the law don't expect to hide behind the law to avoid prosecution.

The building functioned as a courthouse until 1971

when it was turned into an academy for the performing arts. In 1980 it was renamed the **Ernest Cormier Building** and for 28 years was home to the Conservatoire de Musique et d'art dramatique du Québec à Montreal before $38.4-million was spent in 2002 to remodel the art deco interior so the 27 judges of the appeal court court could move back.

All of Montreal's criminal courts were consolidated under one roof when the 17-storey **Palais de Justice** (1 Notre-Dame E.) was built in 1971 at a cost of $40-million. It houses 76 courtrooms.

The small green space between the first and the third courthouse **is Place Marguerite Bourgeoys.** The memorial fountain to the city's first saintly school teacher is the work of **Jules LaSalle.** It depicts Bourgeoys and two children fording a stream. The artist says the statues are meant to show "a woman of courage and energy, a woman of action." Depending on your taste the bronze is either charming or kitsch.

[BETWEEN THE SQUARES]

Champ-de-Mars

A few steps from the **Bourgeoys fountain**, running along the east wall of the **Palais de Justice** is **Baliff's Alley**. Follow it north, head down the stairs, and you will discover the historic Champs-de-Mars, a military parade ground that re-opened as a park in 1992 after being an unsightly parking lot for almost 80 years.

The ruins of the stone walls that you see are all that is left of the stone walls that once surrounded Old Montreal. The city was fortified between 1722 and 1744 by the king's engineer, Gaspard Chaussegros de Léry.

The Champ-de-Mars first appeared on a map of Montreal in 1697 as an orchard for the Jesuit seminary which stood where the city hall is today. With the arrival of a British garrison in 1760 the Jesuits were expelled, and their church became the centre of Protestant worship in Montreal. The new English-speaking community quickly appropriated the gardens as a public promenade. The Lombardy poplars recall the way the park looked in the 19th century.

During the **War of 1812** the field was converted into a military parade ground—Champs-de-Mars—named for the Roman god of war. The city tried to subdivide the property, and happily for future generations, the governor in Quebec City refused. The grounds were, he ruled, "indispensably necessary for the use of the Crown in case it may hereafter be thought fit to occupy it for public purposes."

The Champ-de-Mars was officially designated a public square in 1817. Two years later a visitor to Montreal reported that "Montreal is not of present over burdened with amusements. The principal public amusements are in the assemblies and theatre in the winter and in promenading the Champs de Mars in the summer evenings."

The American writer, **Henry David Thoreau**, watched a military drill there in 1850 and described it as "one of the most interesting sights which I saw in Canada . . . They made on me the impression, not of many individuals, but of one vast centipede of a man."

Through most of the 19th century, the Champ-de-Mars was Montreal's civic square where people gathered to hear political speeches, to attend important civic rallies, and, on occasion to watch public executions. Some of the most militant protest demonstrations in Montreal's history took place on the Champs-de-Mars. The crowd that burned down United Canada's parliament in 1849 gathered on the grounds before it went off to torch the building then located in Place d'Youville. Another angry crowd, most of them women, demonstrated on the Champ-de-Mars on September 6, 1861, after it learned that a Montreal abortionist, James Patterson who had been sentenced to hang, had been reprieved. Patterson was to have gone to the gallows with another man. When news of Patterson's pardon reached Montreal, women took to the streets in a violent protest march demanding Patterson's blood.

Thousands jammed the grounds again in November 1885, to hear a future Prime Minister of Canada, **Wilfrid Laurier,** denounce the hanging of **Louis Riel** who led the Métis uprising in Western Canada.

The Champ-de-Mars was the first site in Montreal to be lit at night by electricity on May 24, 1879 in honour of Queen Victoria's birthday. This enabled the field to be converted into a popular recreation centre after dark. It was flooded every winter after that for years and was dubbed the Prince of Wales Skating Rink.

Champs-de-Mars was paved over in 1913 and became a parking lot shortly afterwards. The last military exercise on the parade ground was on September 11, 1939, ten days after World War II began. Champ-de-Mars was federal government property until 1973 when Ottawa sold the land to the city for $481,000.

In 1990 **Nelson Mandela** was given a tumultuous welcome in the Champ de Mars during his visit to the city. The field was restored in 1992 as part of Montreal's 350th anniversary celebrations.

The building with the six pillars above three arched portals at the east end of the Champ-de-Mars is the **Municipal Courthouse** (at Gosford and St-Louis). It has 13 courtrooms responsible for violations of municipal bylaws—parking tickets, traffic violations and petty theft, and domestic disputes. It was designed as a police station in the Beaux-Arts style by **Omer Marchand**, the first French Canadian to study architecture at the École des beaux Arts in Paris. It opened in 1914, and after Montreal's police headquarters moved to a new location in 1996 the building was completely refurbished in 2000.

Just below City Hall there are two staircases that will take you up to Place Jacques-Cartier (See p. 23) through Place Vauquelin. Between the steps, carved in six panels of granite is the city's **Declaration Against Racial Discrimination.** The declaration, written in French, urges all Montrealers to respect the dignity and rights of everyone, and is meant as denunciation of discrimination, not only against race and people of colour, but also against religious beliefs and sexual orientation.

A translation of the inscription reads:

Whereas the Universal Declaration of Human

Rights and the International Conventions on Human Rights establish the principles of non-discrimination and equality,

And acknowledging that Canada is a signatory and is committed to combat racism and racial discrimination;

Considering that the Quebec Charter of Human Rights and Freedoms upholds these principles and condemns all forms of racism and discrimination,

Determined to encourage all Montrealers to adopt an attitude of respect for human dignity and rights, the Municipal Administration is committed: To take all necessary measures to combat racism based on race, colour, religion, and ethnic or national origin to promote harmonious interracial and intercultural relations in an atmosphere of mutual respect and understanding. Signed in Montreal this 21st Day of March, 1989, Jean Doré Mayor.

Place d'Armes

It is politically incorrect to mention it these days but Place D'Armes acquired its name because it is situated where a small band of European Indian fighters and the city's religious founders first engaged the Iroquois in battle. A plaque on the north side of the square tells the story succinctly: "Near this square, afterwards named Place d'Armes, the founders of Ville-Marie first encountered the Iroquois, whom they defeated, **Paul de Chomedy de Maisonneuve** killing the chief with his own hands, March 1644."

That's de Maisonneuve's statue with the flag, in the centre of the square. Talk of a suitable civic memorial to the city's founders was heard as early as 1879 when the St-Jean Baptiste Society proposed erecting a statue of the Virgin Mary on top of Mount Royal. (Montreal, was after all, originally called Ville-Marie). The city's small but influential Protestant population found that idea offensive, and successfully petitioned against it.

The **de Maisonneuve Monument** was one of several concepts proposed as a compromise. The fundraising campaign for the project didn't get off the ground until 1884, the same year France announced it was giving the Statue of Liberty to the United States. The city's mayor, Honoré Beaugrand hinted that France should do the same for Montreal, After all, de Maisonneuve was born in Neuville-sur-Vanne and is buried in Paris.

No one actually came out and asked France for the gift but expectations were high. First, City Hall chipped in $12,500 to begin the public subscription campaign—an enormous amount of public money for a statue in those

Lambert Clossé with his dog Pilotte, undergoing repairs.

days. Next local sculptor **Louis-Philippe Hébert** was sent to Paris to confer with Frederic Bartholdi, the engineer responsible for the design of the Statue of Liberty. When the French government's contribution came through, however, it amounted to 500 francs. Or, as the papers of the day calculated it, "the disappointingly grand sum of $95.69." Plans for a huge monument to de Maisonneuve were scaled down. The fountain was supposed to be ready for the city's 250th-anniversary celebrations in 1892, but the cornerstone wasn't laid until the following year.

The four figures on the projecting cornices were installed in 1894. They depict Montreal's co-founder, **Jeanne Mance**,who was a headstrong practical nurse; **Lambert Clossé**, de Maisonneuve's second-in-command with his dog, Pilotte; **Charles Le Moyne**, the fur trader who exploited the Indians and who later became seigneur of Longueuil; and the fourth bust is of a generic **Iroquois.**

The four bronze panels depict seminal events from the first 20 years of Montreal's history: the founding of the corporation that engaged de Maisonneuve, the founding mass in 1642; de Maisonneuve's victory over the Iroquois in 1644, and the massacre of Dollard-des-Ormeaux at Long Sault in 1660.

Inscribed on the west side of the monument are de Maisonneuve's words that ring down through history. Warned that he and his followers would be massacred by the Indians if they tried to build a mission on the island, de Maisonneuve replied: "I am determined to go even if every tree on the island turns into an Iroquois." On the east side is the biblical verse, used as the text for the homily preached to the city's 21 founding colonists after the first mass celebrated on May 17, 1642. It is the 19th verse from the 13th chapter of the Gospel of Luke, and prophetically describes Montreal's growth to that of " a mustard seed producing a giant tree."

The monument was unveiled by Quebec's lieutenant-governor, Sir Joseph-Adolphe Chapleau, on July 1, 1895. If you happen to be in town on the closest Sunday to May 17, the anniversary of Montreal's founding, you might want to attend the impressive ceremony held each year in Place d'Armes to mark the occasion.

Place d'Armes was refurbished in 1964 and the de Maisonneuve monument restored in 1990. The formal boundaries of Place d'Armes didn't appear on the map until 1683, at about the same time that Montreal's first parish church went up in the middle of Notre-Dame Street between St-Sulpice and St-François-Xavier streets.

After the British Conquest in 1760 a statue of the British monarch, **George III** dominated the centre of the square but the **American revolutionaries** who occupied the city in 1774 threw it down a well.

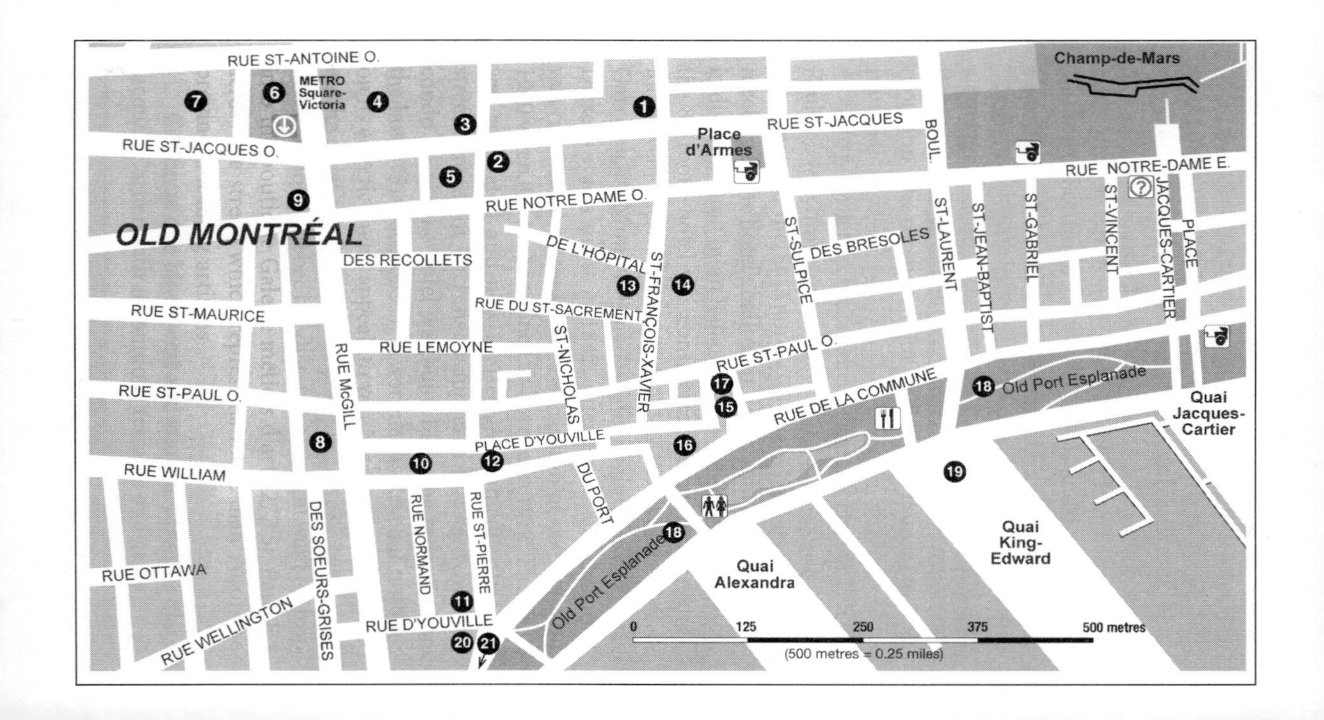
OLD MONTRÉAL
Champ-de-Mars
RUE ST-ANTOINE O.
METRO
Square-
Victoria
RUE ST-JACQUES O.
RUE ST-JACQUES
Place
d'Armes
BOUL.
RUE NOTRE-DAME E.
RUE NOTRE DAME O.
DES RECOLLETS
DE L'HÔPITAL
ST-FRANÇOIS-XAVIER
ST-SULPICE
DES BRESOLES
ST-LAURENT
ST-JEAN-BAPTIST
ST-GABRIEL
ST-VINCENT
PLACE
JACQUES-CARTIER
RUE ST-MAURICE
RUE DU ST-SACREMENT
RUE LEMOYNE
RUE McGILL
ST-NICHOLAS
RUE ST-PAUL O.
RUE DE LA COMMUNE
Old Port Esplanade
Quai
Jacques-
Cartier
PLACE D'YOUVILLE
RUE WILLIAM
DU PORT
DES SOEURS-GRISES
RUE NORMAND
RUE ST-PIERRE
RUE OTTAWA
RUE WELLINGTON
RUE D'YOUVILLE
Quai
Alexandra
Quai
King-
Edward
0
125
250
375
500 metres
(500 metres = 0.25 miles)

OLD MONTREAL
Boulevard St-Laurent West to McGill Street

1. Dominion Express Building
2. Molson Bank Building
3. Hôtel Le St. James
4. World Trade Centre
5. Royal Bank Building
6. Victoria Square
7. Montreal Stock Exchange tower
8. Gérald Godin Building
9. Wilson-Chambers Building
10. Place d'Youville
11. Musée Marc-Aurèle Fortin.
12. Centre d'histoire de Montréal
13. Montreal Telegraph Building
14. Centaur Theatre (Old Stock Exchange)
15. Place Royale
16. Pointe-à-Callière Museum
17. Old Customs House
18. Old Port
19. Montreal Science Centre (King Edward Pier)
20. Allan Building
21. Silo Number 2

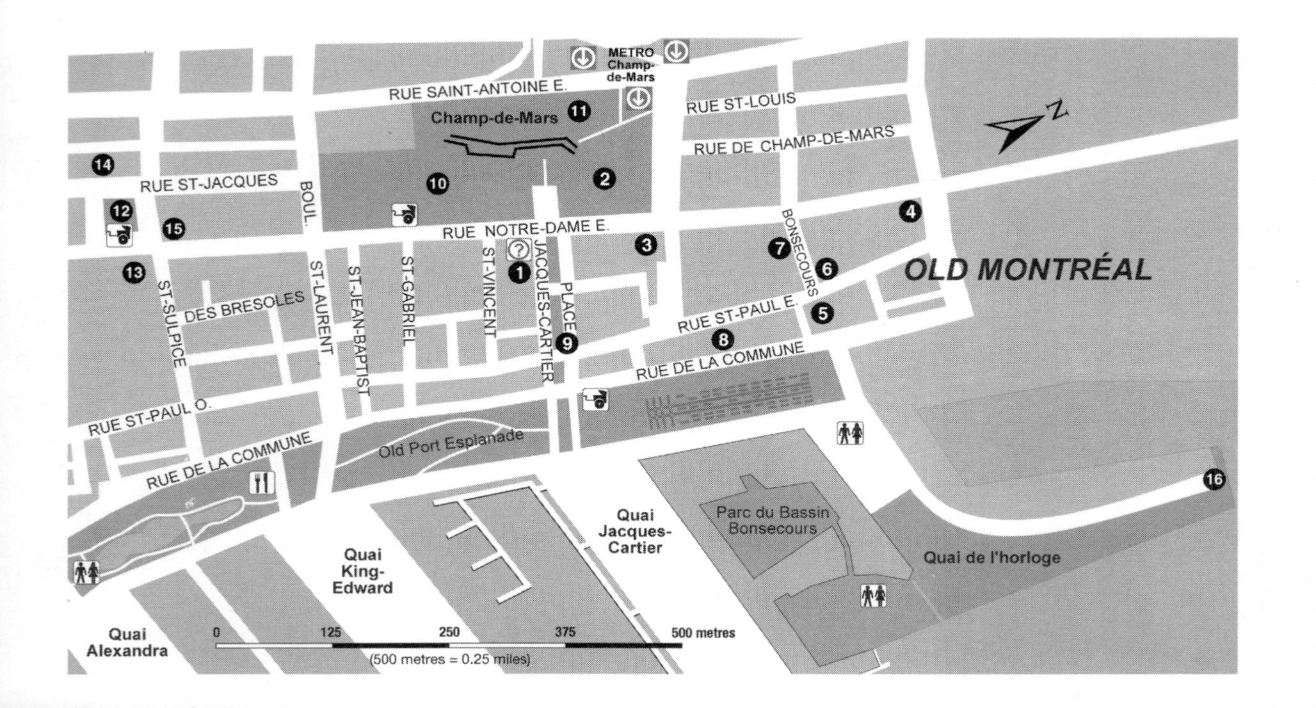
OLD MONTRÉAL
N
METRO
Champ-de-Mars
RUE SAINT-ANTOINE E.
Champ-de-Mars
RUE ST-LOUIS
RUE DE CHAMP-DE-MARS
RUE ST-JACQUES
BOUL.
RUE NOTRE-DAME E.
BONSECOURS
ST-SULPICE
DES BRESOLES
ST-LAURENT
ST-JEAN-BAPTIST
ST-GABRIEL
ST-VINCENT
JACQUES-CARTIER
PLACE
RUE ST-PAUL E.
RUE DE LA COMMUNE
RUE ST-PAUL O.
RUE DE LA COMMUNE
Old Port Esplanade
Quai Jacques-Cartier
Parc du Bassin Bonsecours
Quai de l'horloge
Quai King-Edward
Quai Alexandra
0
125
250
375
500 metres
(500 metres = 0.25 miles)
1
2
3
4
5
6
7
8
9
10
11
12
13
14
15
16

OLD MONTREAL
Boulevard St-Laurent East to Memorial Clock

1. Tourist Information Centre of Old Montreal
2. Montreal City Hall
3. Château Ramezay
4. Sir George-Étienne Cartier National Historic Site
5. Chapelle Notre-Dame-de-Bonsecours
6. Pierre du Calvet House
7. Papineau Residence
8. Bonsecours Market
9. Place Jacques-Cartier
10. Courthouse District
11. Champ-de-Mars
12. Place d'Armes
13. Notre-Dame Basilica
14. Bank of Montreal
15. Aldred Building
16. Sailor's Memorial Clock

The square that evolved is a felicitous mix of old and new. Civic planners consider it one of the greatest urban spaces in North America. It is the only place on the continent encompassed by buildings that represent four centuries of architecture, all of them still occupied.

In spite of its triumphant façade, **Notre-Dame Basilica** on the south side of the square is not a cathedral, Quebec's national shrine, or even a national historic site. It is a parish church and a monastic chapel. But it is no ordinary church. It is revered as a symbol of Montreal and its past, a site filled with more than 300 years of spiritual, cultural and historic French Canadian identity.

An old postcard view of Notre-Dame Basilica.

As a repository of memory, it is where Roman Catholic Montrealers come to be baptized and to be married. It is where in death they are honoured with funerals.

To most people Notre-Dame is familiar as the setting for Luciano Pavarotti's 1979 Christmas special, which is repeated on television every year, as the scene of Quebec pop star's Céline Dion's marriage, or the church from which former Canadian Prime Minister Pierre-Elliott Trudeau was buried.

Notre-Dame's role as a civic shrine is immediately apparent in its 11 stained glass windows created by **Francis Chigot** in Limoges, France and dedicated in 1932. They are unique for a temple. They don't show religious figures but offer a glistening history lesson, depicting important moments in the life of the parish.

It is the second church to occupy the site since the parish was created in 1657. The first, built in 1672, stood directly in Place d'Armes in front of the present church until it was demolished in 1843.

The existing Notre-Dame was built as a political statement by the **Gentlemen of St. Sulpice**, a syndicate of fiercely independent secular priests who were at the time seigneurs of the Island of Montreal. The **Sulpicians** jealously guarded their fief, and objected to interference in their affairs from the Diocesan bishop 300 kilometres away in Quebec City. When the bishop named the malleable Jean-Jacques Lartigue the first bishop of Montreal, the Sulpicians refused to accept the appointment. They threw Lartigue's throne, or cathedra, out of their old church, and in an audacious act designed to reinforce their authority as masters of the island, they decided to build the largest church on the continent.

The Sulpicians hired an Irish Protestant from New York, **James O'Donnell**, to design the church in the

Notre- Dame c. 1976

Gothic style, and contracted James Redpath to build it out of grey limestone. The Jews and Protestants of Montreal donated money toward the cost of its construction.

Although guides often say the church is patterned after Notre-Dame in Paris, it is not. O'Donnell's inspiration, according to church historian Franklin Toker, was St. Martin's in the Fields, and Westminster Abbey, both in London.

Construction began in 1824 and the church opened in 1829. The massive vaulted roof was considered a marvel of advanced engineering at the time, and when Notre-Dame opened it was the largest church building in North America. During the 19th century, it was the second-most-popular tourist attraction in the country after Niagara Falls.

O'Donnell died a convert to Catholicism in 1830 and is the only person buried in the church crypt.

The great **twin towers** he designed are 68 metres tall. (227 ft.) As one stands before the church, the tower to the left is called Temperance, and the one on the right, Perseverance. The main bell, Gros Bourdon, weighs 12 tonnes and is one of the largest in the world. The **three statues** above the doors represent Saint John the Baptist, the patron saint of French Canada, Mary, the patron of Montreal, and Saint Joseph, Canada's patron saint.

Notre-Dame was so costly to build it took another 45 years before enough money was found to decorate it. A self-taught Quebec architect **Victor Bourgeau**, is responsible for the fantastic Prussian blue-and-gold interior, a vast firmament of stars and fleurs-de-lys filled with polychrome, stained glass and hand painted precious wood. French sculptor **Henri Bouriche** carved the **high altar**. Perhaps the most impressive carving in the church, however is Bourgeau's magnificent **pulpit**, with the figures of Old Testament prophets, Jeremiah and Ezekiel.

The **Casavant organ** was installed in 1891 and is considered one of the finest instruments in the city.

Pope John Paul II designated the great Gothic landmark a minor basilica in 1982. The term means "Royal House," and the title is bestowed by the Vatican on churches that have endeared themselves to the community and are especially beautiful. Each evening there is a $3.5-million, 40 minute bilingual sound and light show, that uses the rich interior to tell the history of Montreal and of the church in 22 scenes. (There are two shows each evening at at 6:30 and 8:30. Tickets cost $10.)

Immediately next door is the **Seminaire de St. Sulpice**, the Canadian headquarters for the **Gentlemen of St. Sulpice**. The Sulpicians arrived in 1657 and were given title to the entire island of Montreal in 1663. The central building of the seminary was designed by Dollier de Casson and built in 1684. Someone has lived in apartments on the third floor continuously since then. The clock was added in 1701, the two wings on either side were built in

The head office of the Bank of Montreal. c. 1940, on St. James Street (now St-Jacques).

1705 and a garden at the rear, which is not open to tourists, was laid out in 1715.

The Neo-Classical **Bank of Montreal** on the North side of the square is Canada's first permanent bank. The bank has been around since 1817, but its head office building, the work of Scottish architect **John Wells** resembles the Commercial Bank of Scotland in Edinburgh, and was completed in 1849.

The interior banking hall with is 56-foot high ceiling was decorated in 1905 and is the work of the New York firm **McKim, Mead and White.** It is probably the last major work designed by the notorious and brilliant **Stanford White** before he was shot to death in a lover's quarrel in 1906. Inspired by the churches of Santa Maria Maggiore and San Paolo Fuori, the style is Italian Renaissance. The vast hall features **32 Corinthian columns** of polished green syenite, black Belgian and pink Knoxville marble, gold plated capitals and a richly coffered ceiling. The marble figure wearing a helmet and clutching palm fronds is called Patria, and represents Pietas, the minor Roman god of patriotism. It is a memorial to 231 of the bank's employees killed in World War I, and is the work of American sculptor, James Earle Fraser. It was dedicated in 1928. The statues over the pediment outside deserve a look. The "noble savages" on either side of Montreal's **coat of arms** were carved in Scotland by sculptor John Steell. Obviously, Steell never saw a North American Indian, because if you look carefully, the figure on the right sports a decidedly European-looking mustache. The sailor in the allegorical grouping represents commerce; the settler symbolizes agriculture.

The **Hôtel Place d'Armes** (701 Côte de la Place d'Armes) is a 48-room boutique hotel in an historic Second Empire style building that started life in 1870 as The Great Scottish Life Insurance Building. Designed by John William

Hopkins and Daniel Wiley, it originally had a mansard roof which disappeared when the top three stories were added in 1909. It was declared a historic property in 1975 and converted into a trendy hotel in 2000. Rooms cost between $160 to $225 a night. (514-842-1887).

The red sandstone building directly across the street from the hotel is Montreal's first skyscraper, The **New York Life Insurance Building** which opened in 1889. Its giant face of a clock has been stuck at 1:53 for as long as anyone can remember. Often mistaken as an example of the Chicago School of Architecture, it is in fact the work of a New York architectural firm, Babb, Cook and Willard. Built for $750,000 it was one of the first office buildings to be wired for electricity and the first to be declared fireproof. When the 152 foot-tall Neo-Roman style tower originally opened one newspaper wrote: "It is as if one of those buildings which give a grandeur to the neighbourhood of Broadway and Wall Street were transported by some Aladdin-like process to Montreal." Over the years it has served as head office for the Bank of Quebec, the Banque Canadienne Nationale, and La Société de Fiducie du Québec.

It was acquired in 1976 by an Italian count, Antonio Randacio, president of Compagnie Les Immeubles Bona Ltee. Today it houses the Tunisian Consulate and a medical clinic, as well as bailiffs' offices and the premises of legal and accounting firms.

The 23-story Art Deco **Aldred Building** next door anchors the southwest corner of Place d'Armes. It resembles a wedding cake or a miniature Empire State Building. It was built during the Great Depression by the New York-based Aldred Investment Corp., whose interests in Quebec included the Shawinigan Water and Power Company. The building designed by **Ernest Barott** was inspired by Ralph Walker's New York Telephone Co. building, which created a sensation when it opened in Manhattan in 1926. Barott was careful; he wanted a skyscraper that "would take its place naturally in the historic surroundings." He succeeded. When the building was inaugurated in 1931, it was described as "graceful and dignified, one of the most beautiful structures in the city." Its façade on Place d'Armes is so narrow the floors are stacked away from the square. If you stand by the de Maisonneuve monument and look up, the **Aldred building** appears to be only 15 storeys high. Viewed from the north or south sides, it is massively vertical, free of historic detailing; the only accent is cast aluminum and black glass spandrels which carry the vertical lines skyward. There are two main entrances, (507 Place d'Armes, 85 Notre-Dame W.) which are joined by a functional L-shaped lobby distinguished by a stained glass window and three kinds of marble used on the floors and wainscotting. It is accented by the art deco wall sconces, ventilator grills, filigrees and etched bronze elevator doors. In arched panels overhead, delicate bronze birds drawn by a young architectural student, Lorne B. Marshall, rest on telegraph wires. Outside, a frieze of stylized maple leaves and pine boughs encircles the facade. The building occupies property that was once the home of explorer **Daniel de Greysolon, Sieur Duluth** (1639-1710), but today, you'll find a SAQ liquor store at the corner where his house once stood.

The monstrous black monolith on the west side of the square that casts a black shadow across Place d'Armes went up in 1967 as headquarters for the former Banque Canadienne Nationale. The 32-storey tower was designed to symbolize the dynamic growth of French-Canadian financial interests during the 1960s. It was built by Trizec, the same developer that built Place Ville-Marie.

The Banque Canadienne Nationale merged in the 1970s with another financial institution to form the **National Bank of Canada,** which is committed to lease space on the ground floor of the brutalist skyscraper until 2036. If you meander around to the back, you'll see the bank's maximum-security vault. A freestanding block of black granite outside the building, it seems to float above St-Francois-Xavier Street, the idea being no one can tunnel into it or break through the roof without being seen.

If you take the time to read all the commemorative plaques scattered around Place d'Armes you will learn that in 1837 the Christian Brothers opened their first boys' school where the bank's vault is today, that the city's first well and source of drinking water was dug here, the first law office opened on Place d'Armes in 1683, that explorers La Vérendrye and Daniel Greysolon, Sieur Duluth, had houses nearby, and that foundations of the Montreal School of Medicine, which opened in 1843, aren't far away.

The Aldred Building and Notre Dame Basilica on Place d'Armes.

Rue St-Jacques

Almost all of the buildings along **Rue St-Jacques** were built as banks or brokerage houses in the 19th century when the street was the heart of Canada's financial district.

Rue St-Jacques (or St. James in English) has nothing to do with either of Christ's apostles by that name. It was among one of the first streets to be laid out in the city and is named to remember **Jean-Jacques Olier de Verneuil** (1605-1657) the Sulpician priest who spearheaded the drive to colonize Montreal. The street parallels the foundations of the north wall of the palisade that the French built around Old Montreal in 1685.

The Victorian façades are so splendid the street is regularly used by moviemakers from around the world as a stand-in for 19th century New York, London, or Paris.

As you head west across St. François-Xavier Street, the first building on the south side is the **Dominion Express Building** (201 St-Jacques W.), another in a seemingly infinite number of buildings in Montreal designed by **Edward** and **William Sutherland Maxwell**. The Maxwell brothers designed landmarks across Canada, including the Saskatchewan Legislature, the Palliser Hotel in Calgary, and the Château Frontenac in Quebec City. The Dominion Express Building is the first of four on St-Jacques that they designed.

The 11-storey office building went up in 1912 and replaced the historic St. Lawrence Hall, a hotel in which it was said **John Wilkes Booth** made his plans to kidnap U.S. President Abraham Lincoln. The panels on the Dominion

Express Building were carved by **Leopold Weisz**, an artisan from the Bromsgrove Guild in England who lost his life in the 1912 sinking of the *Titanic*. For many years the Dominion Express Building housed offices for the Banque Nationale du Canada, but was recently remodeled as office space for a high-tech company.

The abandoned building next door with the four columns is where the Royal Bank opened its first head office in Montreal when it moved here from Halifax in 1907. There used to be four heroic sculptures 4.5 metres high representing Manufacturing Mining, Fishing, and Agriculture on the pedestal. Known in their heyday as the Giants of St. James Street, the four limestone figures were taken down in 1989 and can be seen in the Quebec Provincial Archives Building at Viger Square (535 Viger Avenue East).

A few doors along the street you can stop and catch up on the latest news. **The Gazette**, Quebec's only English language daily newpaper posts the front pages of its various sections in its windows each day. *The Gazette* (514-987-2222) is one of the continent's oldest newspapers. It was started by **Fleury de Mesplet** (1734-1794), a French printer from Marseilles who moved to Philadelphia and set up shop before the French Revolution. The Second Continental Congress sent him to Quebec to drum up support in Canada, (then the 14th British colony in North America) for the U.S. revolutionary war. Mesplet was thrown in jail when he arrived in Montreal and after the revolution found himself stuck here with his presses . He began publication of his own newspaper on June 3, 1778. For most of the 20th century *The Gazette* was owned by the conservative White family and was used to advance the family's political views. It lost its competitive edge and its reputation as a journal of record in the early 1990s, a few years before it was acquired by Winnipeg media baron

Izzy Asper. *The Gazette*'s editorial offices are housed in the old *Montreal Star* building which was built in 1899 for the *Montreal Star*, a paper that folded in 1979.

Although the building has been renovated many times, the lobby still boasts its original marble walls and countertops.

The building across the street from *The Gazette* was built in 1902 for the **Guardian Fire and Life Assurance Company** of England (240 St-Jacques W.). Designed by a Chicago firm of architects, Finley & Spence, the excessive stonework is a profusion of lions, garlands, helmeted amazons, and armless sirens. The interior was gutted and completely rebuilt in 1982, but happily, the intricate carvings on the façade remains intact.

The **London and Lancanshire Life Assurance Building** (244 St-Jacques W.) is another of architect **Edward Maxwell**'s designs—his first attempt in the Beaux-Arts style. Canadian financier and British newspaper magnate **Lord Beaverbrook** (1879-1964) once had his offices in the here before he went off to England to become a press baron.

The elegant **XIXe Siècle Hotel** (514-985-0019) which opened at the corner of Rue St- Jean in the spring of 2001 is in building designed in the Beaux-Arts style by Michel Laurent in 1870 for the City and District Savings Bank. The hotel has 60 rooms, and rates range from $200-$325.

Across the street, the massive fortress-like building with the huge columns was built for the **Bank of Commerce** in 1907 and opened in 1909. Its massive pillars are 18 metres high and 2.5 metres thick. In the impressive banking hall is a huge painting by **Adam Sherriff-Scott** that depicts Montreal in the 18th century. The bank is said to be haunted. It stands on what used to be the "heathen" cemetery outside the walls of the city. Five years after the bank opened, ghostly images started to appear in the opalescent windows behind the teller's counter. Nine skulls in the milk glass are visible with the naked eye—look at the second window from the left—and the hall is especially spooky in the late afternoon when the apparition of an old man holding a child in his arms can be seen in the second window from the right.

The **Molson Bank Building** (288 St-Jacques W.) was built in 1866 as a private bank for the Molson family who made its fortune in brewing, steamships and railways. If you look carefully you can see the family's coat of arms and the faces of the bank's founding president, Thomas Molson, and his children carved into the Ohio sandstone arch above the entrance. The bank was absorbed by the Bank of Montreal in 1925, and in 1999 the building was sold to U.S. investors.

Kitty-corner to the Molson Bank is the handsome old **Merchants Bank Building** designed by Hopkins and Wily and built in 1870. It once housed the offices of Nesbitt

The Molson Bank (288 St-Jacques).

Thomson. It is now a 61-room luxury hotel, **Le St. James.** (355 St-Jacques W., 514-841-3111). It stands next door to the **Nordheimer Building** which went up in 1888. The façade was preserved, and the building is now part of the **World Trade Centre** (393 St-Jacques W.). The Nordheimer building has been incorporated into the posh **Inter-Continental Hotel** (360 St-Antoine W., 514-987-9900) which anchors the northeast corner of the World Trade Centre. The airy aitrium inside is worth a look. At the east end there is a **chunk of the Berlin Wall.** The piece weighs 2.5 tonnes and was given to Montreal as a 350th birthday present in 1992 by the City of Berlin. The indoor reflecting pool at the west end of the atrium shows off to advantage a 250-year-old statue of the **sea goddess Amphritite.** Originally the statue by **Dieudonné Barthélemy Guibal** stood in the town square at Meuse in Northern France.

The 29-storey landmark building on the south side of St-Jacques that stands taller than the rest is the **Royal Bank Building** (360 St-Jacques W.). It was designed by **Edward York** and **Phillip Sawyer**, the New York team of architects responsible for the Federal Reserve Bank of New York. They specialized in office buildings, on which they let their considerable inventiveness run riot. The Royal Bank building opened in 1928. The base block houses the banking hall; the tower on top is an office building. Step through the bronze doors into the lavish Italian Renaissance interior with its coffered Wedgewood blue and gold ceiling and you'll realize they just don't build them like this anymore. The intricate ceilings were painted by hand by **Angelo Magnanti**, an Italian craftsman who also worked on the U.S. Supreme Court Building in Washington, D.C. and on the Mormon Temple in Salt Lake City, Utah. The floor is travertine, the walls limestone, and the counter-tops, Levanto marble. The wickets, gates and grills are solid bronze. The coats of arms of Canada's nine provinces at the time, as well as the arms of the cities of Montreal and Halifax (where the bank was founded) are sculpted on the walls just below the ceiling.

In 1957, the bank installed four powerful beacons on the roof, which were moved five years later to the top of Place Ville-Marie.

The Royal Bank Tower on St-Jacques Street, 1930.
When it opened in 1928 it was the tallest building in the British Empire. The British dirigible R100 hovering above it was promoting a transatlantic airship route.

Victoria Square
(International Place)

Queen Victoria has been dead for more than a century but her spirit lives on in Montreal where you can visit not one but three memorials to the 19th century Imperial Empress. The recently refurbished statue to her that stands in International Place was unveiled in 1872. There's another one sculpted by her daughter, Princesss Louise on Sherbrooke St. and yet another one in marble in the Royal Victoria Hospital.

Victoria Square was laid out in 1810 as Square des Commissaires and was commonly referred to as the Hay Market until 1860 when the name was changed to Victoria Square to honor the queen. The statue of her by British sculptor Marshall Wood was raised by public subscription and unveiled on November 21, 1872, by the governor-general, Lord Dufferin as, in his words, "a perpetual ornament and possession to its citizens and to their descendants forever."

The perpetual ornament has been moved around many times and even though in recent years it has been defaced with graffiti, vandalized, and even bombed as a symbol of a British colonial dominance, it still stands.

A century ago, Victoria Square was almost three times the size it is today—a jewel-like acre of green space with a splashing fountain. By the 1870s it was the heart of Montreal's financial district enclosed by department stores, furniture display rooms, a hotel, and the YMCA.

Although you won't find any reminder of it, Victoria Square was the scene of the only bloody clash between

Catholics and Protestants in the city. It occurred July 12, 1877 during an Orange parade, when Thomas Lett Hackett, 22, was killed here.

The bucolic character of Victoria Square began to be transformed in the 1930s. Developers began improving the area by demolishing it. The only reminder from the Victorian era is the greystone facade of the **Douglas-McIntyre Building** (751 McGill) that was built in 1875. Today it's the corporate headquarters of Power Corporation, and is part of the World Trade Centre (*See page* 55) which opened on the east side of Victoria Square in April 1992.

The first of the modern office buildings to be built on Victoria Square is the **Bank of Canada Building** (901 McGill) which opened as the Bank of Canada in 1949. It closed in 1991 and in 2001 was incorporated into the new headquarters of the Caisse de Dépôt et Placement du Québec.

In the early 1950s, the **Toronto Dominion Bank** and the **Bank of Nova Scotia** erected new buildings on the south-east corner. The decorative frieze above the main entrance of the TD Canada Trust building (500 St-Jacques W.) is the work of a Romanian-born artist, Joseph Illiu. The panels represent Quebec architecture, early settlers of Eastern Canada, Jacques Cartier, Quebec arts and crafts, Paul Chomedey de Maisonneuve, and the province's natural resources.

In 1961, the **Imperial Bank** built a 15-storey tower across the street from the TD bank. After the Imperial Bank merged with the Bank of Commerce, the building was used by various trust companies until 1986 when the French-language media giant, **Québecor**(612 St-Jacques) moved its corporate headquarters here. In the summer of 1999 the French-language television network, Télèvision Quatre Saisons began broadcasting from street level

Victoria Square in better days.

television studios in the building.

The **Montreal Stock Exchange** tower (800 Victoria Square) that soars on the west side of the square is the work of two Italian engineering architects, **Pier Luigi Nervi** and **Luigi Moretti**. When it opened on October 21, 1965, critics hailed it as a "poem in concrete."

It is one of what were supposed to be two identical towers, but the second phase was never built. Instead, a hotel was added. Side by side, the two buildings offer an object lesson in architecture. The difference between architectural excellence and mediocrity is evident at a glance.

When the 47-storey skyscraper went up, most of Victoria Square was reduced to a concrete terrace at its base. Then the métro and the Ville Marie Expressway were cut under it. An unsightly ventilation tower built in 1973 was the final blow—Victoria Square became too forbidding to be friendly. In 1986 more than a million dollars was spent planting trees and adding a fountain, but it remained empty.

Victoria Square was torn up again the summer of 2000, and is once again being realigned. $12-million is being spent to return the public space to its original configuration. The historic statue of the queen will be returned to its original location, four granite reflecting pools will be built, and a new entrance to the métro is planned. It will be decorated with an elegant green iron Art Nouveau grille and two lamp posts created in 1900 by **Hector Guimard**, a leading French exponent of art noveau in architecture. The railings were given by the City of Paris to Montreal as a Canadian centennial gift in 1967. Two other monuments—one to **Joseph Xavier Perrault**, the founder of the Chambre de Commerce, the other to the **Salvation Army**, have been relocated to an island in front of the **Place Victoria** skyscraper. Work is expected to be finished in the spring of 2003.

McGill Street

McGill Street below St-Jacques isn't the most pedestrian-friendly block in the city, but there are a exceptional sites to see in the area including the handsome façade of Victorian buildings along its west side

As you might suspect, the street is named for **James McGill** (1744-1813) the fur trader and founder of McGill University. McGill supervised the demolition of the walls that surrounded the old city and when he died unexpectedly, the road along the west wall of the fortifications was named in his memory.

In the distance, at the end of the street you can see **Silo Number 5**, the only remaining grain elevator in the Old Port. Built in 1903 and abandoned in 1994, the elevator with its cubic, spherical, and cylindrical proportions was once considered avant-garde architecture. Its the focus of a debate between preservationists who want to see it refurbished, and those who want it torn down because they consider it an eyesore.

As you head towards it, you will pass the **Soto Sushi** restaurant (514-864-5115) situated on the ground floor of the **Wilson-Chambers Building** (500 McGill). The building dates from 1868, and was built by hardware merchant **Senator Charles Wilson** (1808-1877), Mayor of Montreal between 1851-54. The building, renovated in 1990, is a gem. It is one of the few Victorian commerical buildings in the city with inventive architectural flair. Designed by **Richard Windeyer**, it combines the Gothic with the Second Empire style.

The Gérald Godin Building was originally built by *Titanic* passenger Charles Hays, president of the Grand Trunk Pacific Railroad.

The building at 460 McGill houses the offices of the alternative weekly, *The Mirror*.

The **Gérald Godin Building** (360 McGill) is named for a highly-respected poet and politician (1938-1994) who was once a minister of immigration in the Quebec Government. Originally the building opened in 1902 as headquarters for **the Grand Trunk Railway**. The Grand Trunk was a British company, with corporate headquarter in London. For the first half century of its existence in Canada, local operations were managed out of a series of makeshift offices, first in Point St. Charles, then in the Nelson Hotel on Place Jacques Cartier. That changed in

1896. Faced with stiff competition from the Canadian Pacific Railway, the Grand Trunk hired **Charles Melville Hays**, away from the Wabash, St. Louis and Pacific Railway, to bring American savvy to bear upon the GTR's stagnating fortunes. One of Hays's first priorities was to expand the line. The other was to build a corporate headquarters to house the company's 500 Canadian employees. The company's president in London, Sir Charles Rivers Wilson, wanted something functional. Hays opted for something grander—a building that would stand as a testament to the Grand Trunk's future.

Hays got his way. He hired **Richard Waite**, a Buffalo, N.Y., architect and a leading interpreter of the Beaux-Arts style, who also designed Ontario's Parliament Buildings, Queen's Park, in Toronto. Waite's original design incorporated a copper dome over the north tower, but the dome was never completed. Originally, the building was to cost $550,000. Almost twice that amount was spent before it was finished, most of it on the lavish stone interior which is decorated with seven shades of marble imported from Belgium, France, Italy Greece Egypt, and the United States. The basement and ground floor of Stanstead granite and the upper stories of Indiana limestone are deceptive. Inside, there is an explosion of space and rich appointment. The business offices open onto a central court 27 metres high, illuminated by a vast skylight. Waite's trademark sculptures are an integral part of the design. Gryphons, symbolizing strength and speed, grace the north tower and flank the main staircase. Charles Melville Hays drowned in the sinking of the *Titanic* in 1912. Seven years later The Grand Trunk Railroad went bankrupt and in 1923 the company was placed under the management of the Canadian National Railway. The building was used as CN's head office until 1961, when it was sold to the Quebec government. It was completely remodelled and stripped of much of its original marble and Victorian extravagance. Eight ornate marble fireplaces in the old executive suites are, however, still there. Today it houses the Montreal offices of the Ministère de Communautés Culturelles et de l'Immigration.

Directly opposite is the **Hôtel St-Paul** (355 McGill, 514-380-2222) which opened in the summer of 2001. It is in the old **Canadian Express Building** which went up in 1900 as headquarters of the Canadian transport and financial company that rivaled American Express. It is where the Grand Trunk Railway across the street processed its international money transfers. The building was designed by architect **Alexander Hutchison** (1838-1921) the son of the Scots stonemason who also designed McGill University's Redpath Museum and the Erskine and American United Church. The strong exterior of the building inspired the use of simple materials when the sparse interior of the building was converted into a hotel. Each of the 120 rooms in the new luxury hotel are almost monastic in their chic simplicity and feature two twin line phones, a CD player, and access to a fibre-optic computer network. Rooms rates range between $230 and $350 a night. **Cube**, the hotel's restaurant, offers a creative menu which is simple yet attractive, in keeping with the stark minimalist decor.

Next door, to the north of the hotel is the **Shaughnessy Building** (401 McGill) erected in 1912 as offices for the Canadian Pacific Railway. It was sensitively designed by the New York firm of **McKim, Mead and White** to blend into the streetscape and to compliment the Canadian Express Building next door.

Place d'Youville

There is nothing to indicate it today but The Canadian Parliament once stood in the parking lot that sprawls across much of the west end of **Place d'Youville** immediately south of the Hotel St. Paul.

Montreal became the capital of The United Province of Canada in 1844 and the government moved into St. Ann's Market, an imposing two-storey limestone building that was built here in the early 1830s. The marketplace, 350 feet long and 50 feet wide, was converted into an imposing House of Assembly. The Legislative Council was in the east wing, the House of Assembly occupied the west wing. **John A. Macdonald**, later Canada's first prime minister, made his maiden speech as a parliamentarian in the building on April 27, 1846.

The first experiment in joint government between English and French, however, ended in disaster. Montreal might have remained the national capital to this day had a booze-soaked Anglo mob not torched the parliament building on April 25, 1849. Inflamed by incendiary editorials in *The Gazette* the crowd marched on the building to show its anger at legislation passed by the assembly which would have required the Crown to compensate French Canadians for damages caused by the British Army during the Rebellion of 1837.

All that was saved from the fire was the legislative mace, and a portrait of Queen Victoria which now hangs in the lobby outside the Senate Chamber in Ottawa. As a result of the violence Montreal lost its status as capital of Canada, and the seat of government alternated between Quebec City and Toronto until 1858 when Queen Victoria settled on Ottawa as the capital. A second market—"a queer pagoda like building"—was built on the same site in 1851, expanded in 1871 and burned in 1893. The walls were demolished in 1901 and the square was named Place d'Youville in honour of **St. Marguerite de Lajemmerais d'Youville** (1701-1771), founder of the Sisters of Charity, commonly known as the **Grey Nuns**. She is the first Canadian-born saint, and was canonized by the Vatican in 1994.

The huge neo-classical building with splendid arched doorways on the south side of the parking lot is the **Canada Customs House** (400 Place d'Youville), which was the setting for the heist in *The Score,* the recent movie starring Robert De Niro and Marlon Brando. The first three floors are faced in granite, and the floors above that, sandstone. It was built in stages by the Ministry of Public Works between 1912 and 1936. There is a vast and impressive central hall inside, as well as a small display on the history of Canada Customs.

Across Normand Street to the east is where Montreal's first hospital, the Hôpital Général was built in 1693 and was taken over by the Grey Nuns under the direction of Mother d'Youville in 1747. The hospital burned in 1765 and was rebuilt. The stone walls that you see date from the 18th century building. The buildings were partially restored in 1971, and the room where **Marguerite d'Youville** died is preserved as a sanctuary. It is not open to the public. The sisters still use the buildings as their administrative head office. The original chapel was torn down in 1872 when the Grey Nuns moved uptown into the convent at the corner of Guy Street. and René-Lévesque Boulevard, but some of its walls that once enclosed the transept of the chapel still stand on Rue St. Pierre. Interpretive panels include the script of the letters patent signed by Louis XIV establishing the hospital and the monument gives you some idea of what the hospital complex looked like 200 years ago.

Just beyond the ruins of the hospital's old chapel is the **Musée Marc-Aurèle Fortin** (118 St. Pierre, 514-845-6108). Fortin (1888-1970) a prolific painter of robust Quebec landscapes and massive trees, painted about 10,000 works, most of which were destroyed or lost after he was hospitalized in 1967. Mistreated during his lifetime, this museum dedicated to his paintings opened in 1984.

The plaque at 224 St. Pierre marks the site of first **Governor's Mansion** built by **Louis Hector de Callières**, (1648-1703) who was acting governor of New France from 1698 to 1703. Callières left his mark on history by making peace with the Iroquois in 1701. His mansion was built in 1688 and after the British conquest in 1760 fell into ruins and was left to deteriorate. The walls were torn down at the beginning of the 19th century.

At 298 St. Pierre you will find old warehouses that have been converted into upscale condos and office space. The courtyard, with its ivy covered walls is always inviting. The first door to the left as you walk through the gates is **Gibby's** (514-282-1837), Montreal's most popular steak house. It's not the city's best steak house but its stone walls, low ceilings, wood beams and fireplace project enough warmth and old world ambiance that the regulars keep coming back. Gibby's has been around for 30 years, and word of mouth has made it one of those places you have try just to say you have been there. Reservations should be booked well in advance.

The red brick building directly across the street from Gibby's, on an island in the middle of Place d'Youville, is the the old Number One Fire Station. It was built in 1903 and in 1983 was converted into the **Centre d'histoire de Montréal** (335 Place d'Youville, 514-872-3207), a civic museum. The interior was completely refurbished in 2001 and the new exhibition space is filled with nostalgia. Typical daily life in a typical Montreal family in days gone by. You can hear snippets of **Hockey Night in Canada broadcasts**, listen to a recitation of the rosary, or take a simulated tram ride on an old Montreal street railway car. The main floor features an exhibit called five windows on history, and each of the five alcoves has a theme dealing with the development of Montreal. Among the treasure trove of civic memorabilia you can find the baseball bat used by **Jackie Robinson** when he played for the **Montreal Royals** in 1947 and the first contract **Maurice 'Rocket' Richard** signed in 1942 with the Montreal Canadiens for $5,000 a season. A small gallery on the third floor houses a circulating exhibition, and to get to it you have to go through a glassed in walkway on the roof that offers visitors yet another panoramic view of Old Montreal. Admission is $6.25 for adults, $5.50 for seniors and students. The area behind the Centre d'Histoire is known as **Place de la Grand Paix**, named in honour of the Great Peace of Montreal, a treaty signed on the same spot in 1701 between the French and 39 aboriginal nations.

The accord was more of a truce than a lasting peace treaty; but it did outfox the British in the New England colonies, allowed the French to expand their frontiers west to the Great Lakes and down the Mississippi, and effectively ended almost a century of hostilities that often threatened to wipe Montreal off the map.

The stylized playful and poetic metal cross immediately behind the old fire hall is a **sculpture** by **Gilles Mihalcean** called "L'oeuvre." It symbolizes the origins of the French-speaking Roman Catholic Church in America. It was installed in 1993.

Look east and you will see a **grey granite obelisk.** It is dedicated to Montreal's founders, the original 35

This granite obelisk was erected in 1894 to honour Montreal's founders who arrived from France in 1642.

colonists who arrived from France in 1642. The obelisk is made from a block of granite that stands 41 feet tall and is three feet square at its base. It weights 22-tonnes, and is said to be the largest piece of stone ever quarried in Canada. It took 40 horses to drag the shaft into the city in 1893. The monument was erected in May, 1894, and has been moved a number of times before it was placed in its present location in 1999.

Landscape architect Claude Cormier's interpretive design for Place d'Youville is meant to suggest a quilt; a single whole stitched together from many many historic elements. The granite walkway through the centre makes reference to an underground stream, the Little St. Pierre River which was vaulted over in 1832. Wooden walk-ways cross from domestic door to domestic door and ankle high granite fencing and waist high lighting symbolize four centuries of movement through the square. Cormier has also a designed a treatment for the parking lot in the west section of Place d'Youville where the Parliament once stood, but it has not yet been adopted.

St-François-Xavier Street

One of the pleasures of meandering through Old Montreal is exploring its side streets and stumbling across the unexpected. Heading up **St-François-Xavier Street** gives you a compact slice of the city's cosmopolitan character. Squeezed into its three short blocks are Korean, Mexican, Polish, and Italian restaurants. The street is one of the oldest in the city. Originally when it was laid out in 1678 is was called St-François, for **François Dollier de Casson** (1636-1701), Superior of the Sulpicians. In the middle of the 18th century the street also honoured the the saint who founded the **Jesuit order**, François-Xavier, (1506-1552). The first restaurant on your left is a simple, inexpensive, but good little seafood cafe, **Le Bourlinguer** (363 St-François-Xavier, 514-845-3646). Directly across the street, is **Stash Café** (200 St. Paul W., 514-845-6611)) which specializes in hearty Polish cusine.

The exuberant building at 422-24 St-François-Xavier is the **Montreal Telegraph Building** which went up in 1873 as Canada's communications clearing house. All telegrams sent throughout the country were processed here. There used to be a cupola that looked like a pepper mill on the false mansard roof , but it was removed in the 1920s.

Auberge Bonaparte and its restaurant (447 St-François-Xavier, 514-844-1448) began in 1984 as a restaurant, and in 1999 it opened 30 guest rooms. There are three dining rooms; the formal Impératrice, the airy La Serre, and the Centre Room. No two guest rooms are the same, and rates range between $150 and $200 a night. If you stay here, try and book one of the rooms in the rear that overlook the Sulpican's garden. There's also a suite with a private terrace that goes for $300 a night. Directly across the street is the **Casa de Matéo Auberge** and restaurant (438 St-François-Xavier, 514-286-9589). The 20 rooms are inexpensive by Montreal standards—$80 a night, but you might be kept awake on weekends by the mariachi band that plays in the restaurant downstairs.

Next door, at the corner of de l'Hôpital Street. is the **Canadian Pacific Telegraph Chambers Building** (444 St-François-Xavier), which was built in 1900 as the telegraph centre linking Toronto with Quebec City and the Maritimes.

The **Canadian Stock Exchange** building (453 St-François-Xavier), with its six Corinthian columns that looks like a Greek temple, was built in 1903. New York architect **George Post**, who designed a mansion for Cornelius Vanderbilt II on Fifth Avenue in Manhatten took as his inspiration for the stock exchange the Temple of Vesta in Tivoli. The side wings were added in 1928. The last shares were traded in the building on October 21, 1965. It was converted into a cultural centre in 1967, and the **Centaur Theatre**, the city's professional resident English language theatre company, took over the building in 1969. In 1972 they converted it into two theatres. The larger theatre seats 425, the smaller, 255. To find out what's playing or to make reservations, call 514-288-3161.

Look at the lintel above the window at 480 St. François-Xavier and you will see the word "Fairyland" carved into the stone. The building now houses **Ponton**, which has been supplying costumes since1865. Next to it is the **British Empire Building** (482 St-François-Xavier) designed by **John William Hopkins** in 1874 which once housed the Exchange bank. The site of the Empire Building is of interest because in the 1670s Montreal's first tavern was stood here. It was run by a notorious cabaretière, **Anne Lamarque** (1648-1686), who earned the nickname La Folleville. Running a tavern in the 17th century was no job for a woman, and the place earned a reputation as a disorderly house where gambling, drunkeness, and brawling were rampant. In 1682, La Folleville was charged with being a witch and a sorceress, and was convicted and banished from Montreal. Her spirit endures. Someone should mark the site with a plaque.

Place Royale

Nowhere is Old Montreal's new face more apparent than in the Place Royale, the city's first public square. Here a 1992 modernist monument, architect **Dan S. Hanganu**'s **Pointe-à-Callière Museum of Archeology and History** (350 Place Royale, 514-872-9150) and the historic **Customs House** (151 de la Commune St. W.) face each other across a slab of concrete that covers hallowed ground.

It was on this very spot that Montreal's founder, **Paul de Chomedey**, Sieur de Maisonneuve and his fellow colonists landed 360 years ago on May 16, 1642 and built the first stone mission originally named Ville-Marie de Montréal. The exposed wooden foundations of the original stockade and the graves of a few of those first colonists are in the museum's basement where some of the skeletons of those buried here between 1643 and 1654 can be seen.

Exhibits upstairs include thousands of items found in archeological digs around the city including Indian pottery, harpoons, and arrow heads dating back to the year 1000. There is also a 15-minute multi-media presentation, "Montreal, Tales of a City." It's an entertaining, if sanitized, history lesson that uses film, holograms and live actors to condense thousands of years into an 18-minute show. After your tour, check out the belevedere and the rooftop restaurant with their panoramic view of the harbour.

The $27.5-million museum was built to commemorate Montreal's 350th birthday in 1992. Regular visiting hours are 10 a.m. to 5 p.m. Tuesday and Thursday through Sunday, and 10 a.m. to 10 p.m. Wednesday. It is closed on

Custom House, Place Royale, 1860.

Mondays. $6 for adults, $5 for seniors, $3 for students 13 to 18 and free for children 12 and under.

The huge brass urn on the steps outside the museum, by the way, has not fallen from its pedestal. It's part of a **sculpture**, "Entre Nous," by **Andrew Dutkewych**, which is meant to be a metaphor in bronze for the city's cultural riches.

The Museum of Archeology faces Montreal's oldest public square, the **Place Royale**, now brutally paved with a forbidding expanse of granite. Engraved on the surface is a rather obsolete observation about the city from *Picturesque Canada*, an 1882 guidebook by Rev. A. J. Bray and John L'Esperance: "There can be no more beautiful city on the continent of America that the commercial metropolis of the Dominion of Canada. Lying between the river and Mount Royal. Rarely has it been the good fortune of any city to have so fine a background....."

A translation of the French words inscribed on the plaza, taken from Dollier de Casson's 1672 *History of Montreal*, reads, "If you are looking for a convenient place to trade, since this is as far as boats can come up the river, it is the ideal spot to meet with the trappers and traders who can bring their goods here from the interior."

The Neo-Classical building overlooking the square is the old **Customs House**, which dates from 1836. It is one of the first public buildings in the city to be designed by a professional architect, in this case by **John Ostell**. It looks much the same from the outside today as it did when it was built, but the interior was remodelled in 1988, and now it serves as the Pointe-à-Callière museum's gift shop and bookstore.

Take the first narrow street to the left of the old Customs House. It looks like a back alley, but is really **Rue de la Capitale**. Halfway down the street you will come to **Ruelle Chagouamigon**, which is only about 20 feet long. In the 17th century, aboriginals were, for reasons of security, not permitted inside the walls of the stockade. The street was originally the west wall of the wooden stockade and is so named because in the 1680s it was where traders from Fort Chagouamigon on the shores of Lake Superior plied their wares when they came to Montreal.

Rue de la Commune

Rue de la Commune means The Common, but there is nothing common about the streetscape. Before 1990, rue de la Commune was the Montreal waterfront, a run-down strip of warehouses and factories, along a raw, industrial market area. The architectural façade along the street hasn't changed all that much over the past century and a half, but the neighbourhood has. Rue de la Commune grew out of what was once a livestock pasture used by the colonists who built **Ville-Marie mission** on the banks of the St. Lawrence River in 1642. It runs for 2 kilometres and it has been a public promenade since the city's early days. On the first warm day of the new year, the settlers would leave their little stockade and walk along the riverbank. When Montreal grew into a fortified town, fur traders beached their canoes along the common each spring and congregated along the walls by rue de la Commune, where they set up camp and held rowdy trade fairs.

Once the city's stone walls were torn down after the **War of 1812**, an attempt was made to re-christen rue de la Commune as Water Street, but the name never took. In the 1930s urban planners talked of plowing a six-lane elevated expressway through rue de la Commune, but wiser heads prevailed. The neighbourhood began to be transformed when the federal government tore down a huge, concrete grain elevator in 1978 to open "a window on the St. Lawrence," and turned 54 hectares into a federal presence in the city. The park known as the **Old Port** opened on June 23, 1981, and in the past 20 years $200 million has been spent to convert the green space between

The Allan Building. This is where the message that the *Titanic* had hit an iceberg and was sinking was received.

the river and rue de la Commune into a people place, a recreational waterfront.

Unlike some other waterfront redevelopments the Old Port has retained its maritime character. Hulking Great Lakes freighters and cruise ships and yachts are berthed along the wharf that stretches for two and a half kilometres.

Perhaps the best place to begin a tour is at the foot of the statue of **John Young** at the corner of Youville and St-Pierre streets. Young (1811-1878) was the first chairman of the Montreal Harbour Commission, who in the 19th century transformed Montreal's seaport from a third-class wharf into an international harbour. His statue by sculptor **Louis-Phillipe Hébert** stands above a recently-restored fountain, which includes a figure of Neptune rising from the sea.

Young's statue is in front of the **Allan Building** (333 de la Commune), completed in 1858 as headquarters for the Allan Steamship Line, which provided transatlantic mail service between Montreal and Liverpool, England. The Italianate-style, Neo-Renaissance building was restored in 1983 and today houses the offices of the Canada Lands Company, the crown corporation responsible for the development of the Old Port. It was in this building that the message that the *Titanic* had hit an iceberg and was sinking in 1912 was first received in Montreal and relayed to the world.

The building directly to the left and behind it is the old **Harbour Commissioners' Building**. It was built in 1875 for the Harbour Commission which controlled navigation on the St. Lawrence River until the St. Lawrence Seaway was built in the 1950s. Designed in the second Empire style by Alexander Cowper Hutchison, the building burned in 1997 and is being restored by high tech magnate Daniel Langlois as the headquarters for his foundation which promotes the use of new technology in the arts.

There is no plaque to indicate it but the building at 207 de la Commune, where the legendary Montreal character **Charles McKiernan** (aka Joe Beef) opened his notorious tavern in 1870. **Joe Beef's saloon** was a wild place in its Victorian heyday, with a human skeleton behind the bar and a live bear on the premises. When Joe Beef ran it, story has it that no one in need was turned away hungry or without a bed for the night. McKiernan died in 1889, but the tavern he started didn't close its doors until 1982.

Head east across the Place Royale, and if you want to buy a model of the Bluenose or any other sailing ship, pop into **Les Forges Fantastique** (131 rue de la Commune). A few doors away is **Café Hélios** (117 rue de la Commune), an inexpensive cappuccino bar in a 130-year old building that was once the site of a tough waterfront bar called The Neptune. The house specials, all under $10, include

A view of Rue de la Commune in the days of sail.
The dome of Bonsecours Market can be seen in the distance.

include an Apollo, a Zorba and a Mythos—fancy names for smoked salmon, a croque monsieur, and a chicken sandwich. Next door is the **Auberge de la Place Royale** (115 de la Commune, 514-287-0522), a rustic 11-room inn. Rates range between $175 and $300 a night and include a complimentary breakfast.

If you would rather roller blade than walk, Montréal en Ligne Plus (55 rue de la Commune) is one of three outlets along the street where you can rent **in-line skates** or even **bicycles** ($15 for 2 hours). The others are Ça Roule(27 rue de la Commune E.) and Velocité (99 St-Laurent Blvd.). St-Laurent divides the addresses in Montreal, and on rue de la Commune, into east and west.

One of the main attractions along the street is the **Montreal Science Centre** (King Edward Pier), the long, sleek glass buildings in the **Old Port** on the south side of the street. You can't miss it. Its flashy electronic sign is an eyesore in the neighbourhood, but its virtual games, inter-

The city viewed from the Old Port.

active science activities, technological exhibits and immersion theatre —part movie, part giant-size video game— offer stimulating entertainment for the whole family.

The complex also includes an Imax Theatre and a restaurant. If you pass on the ISCI centre, and continue along rue de la Commune you will come to an inviting hole-in-the-wall, **Crème de la Crème Café.** Two doors down is another bistro, **Pops Crêpes and Creme,** and next door, **Kilimanjaro** (514- 875-2332), a bistro that specializes in bruschetta, nachos and North African-style grilled pizza, all for under$10.

The 27-room **Auberge du Vieux Port** (97 rue de la Commune E., 514-876-0081) was a leather factory for more than a century before it was converted into a romantic hideaway with a river view. **Hector Lamontagne** opened the factory in 1882. When his descendants closed the operation in 1989 they discovered the founder's safe which too heavy to move. So there it still sits, in use, behind the hotel's reception desk. There's a rooftop terrace that's worth a stop. It's a hideaway above the crowds, with a **panoramic view** of the Old Port and the marina. To get there, take the elevator to the 5th floor and walk up one flight of stairs. Its a small space—only 14 tables. **Les Remparts** restaurant (93 rue de la Commune, 514-392-1649) in the hotel basement, is one of the best along the street. It's a cave-like room with cut stone walls. It offers excellent traditional French cuisine with a contemporary flair. Further along is the stage door to **Le Pierrot** (front entrance at 104 St Paul), a popular popular boîte-à-chanson.

You won't find a ubiquitous McDonald's or a Second Cup along rue de la Commune, but if you are in the mood for fast food, there are the three take-out places between 127 and 133 rue de la Commune—**Queues de Castor**, which offers beaver tails (deep fried dough with different toppings); **Moozoo** (soft ice cream and milk shakes), and **Frites Alors**, (real French fries served with mayonnaise). The Dépanneur du Fiacre, sells soft ice cream, but everything else inside is over-priced.

If you want a caléche ride—the horse-drawn carriages can usually be found directly across the street, lined up on the south side of rue de La Commune at the foot of Place Jacques Cartier. Its costs $30 for a half hour. If you would rather skip the ride, head through the gates towards the **Pavillion Jacques-Cartier**, an information centre that will keep you posted on all the activities on the Old Port's 20th anniversary program. Behind the information centre is a marina. You can catch a ferry to **Parc Jean-Drapeau** across the river, or book a 3½-hour dinner cruise on the glass-enclosed *Bateau Mouche* which leaves each evening at 7 p.m.

Head east from the information centre along the wharf and walk past **Bonsecours Basin**, a skating rink in winter and an outdoor pool with pedal boats in summer. The exposed foundations you see are all that remain of

Silo Number 2, one of the world's largest grain elevators that was built in 1912 and torn down when the park was created. A couple of boats in the Old Port still offer the simple pleasure of a cruise down the river, and you willfind them at the end of your walk. Just how far downstream you go depends on which excursion you choose.

Groupe AML operates a choice of **cruises** until the Thanksgiving Day weekend in early October. These include a 3½ -hour, 50-kilometre sunset dinner cruise; Sunday breakfast cruises; and short, leisurely luncheon cruises around the harbour.

For the more adventurous, the jet boats of Saute Moutons (514-284-9607) run the Lachine rapids. Evening dinner cruises are offered on AML's largest vessel, *Cavalier Maxim*. It has five decks on four levels, and three dining rooms. Le Verrier on A Deck can accommodate 180 passengers; Club Maxim on B Deck seats 285; and the Salle Panoramique, a gourmet dining room under a glass dome on C Deck, has room for 235. A smaller boat, *MV Montreal*, mainly cruises the harbour. *Cavalier Maxim* boards each evening at 6:30 and sails at 7 p.m. from Alexandra Pier for the 3½-hour dinner cruise. The *MV Montreal* leaves from the Jacques Cartier Pier for the two-hour luncheon cruise around the harbour. For information on sailings, group rates and reservations, call 514-842-3871.

All cruises sail past the **Sailor's Memorial Clock**, at the extreme east end of the Old Port. The clock commemorates the Canadian sailors and merchant mariners who died in two World Wars. The cornerstone for the 147-foot-tall tower was laid by the **Prince of Wales** , October 31, 1919, and it was completed two years later. There are 192 steps to the observation deck, but the tower is being refurbished and realigned to eliminate a slight tilt.

Index of People and Places

Index of Restaurants

Index of Web Sites

Hôtel Place d'Armes
www.hotelplacedarmes.com

Hôtel St. Paul
www.hotelstpaul.com

Hour Magazine
www.hour.qc.ca

IMAX Theatre of the Old Port
www.imaxoldport.com

Le Fripon
wwwlefripon.com

Les Forges Fantastique
www.adiken.com

Marriott SpringHill Suites
www.springhillsuites.com

Montreal Gazette
www.canada.com/montreal/montrealgazette

Montreal International Airport
www.admtl.com

Montreal Science Centre
www.isci.ca

Pointe-à-Callière Museum of Archeology and History
www.musee-pointe-a-calliere.qc.ca

Tourist Information Centre of Old Montreal
www.tourism-montreal.org

Véhicule Press
www.vehiculepress.com

Via Rail Canada
www.viarail.ca

Photo Credits

Cover, 2 Alan Hustak, 12 Alan Hustak, 14 old postcard, 17 Alan Hustak, 19 George Fenyon, 24 unknown, 36 Alan Hustak, 42 old postcard, 44 Tedd Church, 46 unknown (Bank of Montreal Archives), 50 Batten Limited (1930), 54 Alan Hustak; 56 unknown (Royal Bank Corporate Archives); 59 old postcard, 62 Alan Hustak, 69 Alan Hustak, 75 Notman Photographic Archives, 78 Alan Hustak, 80 Public Archives of Canada (PA149728), 81 Alan Hustak.

For updates on the Walking Tours of Montreal

visit us on the Web.

Go to "Tour Updates"

www.vehiculepress.com